This
Book
Belongs
To _

Grolier Enterprises Inc.
SHERMAN TURNPIKE, DANBURY, CONNECTICUT 06816

Book Club Edition

The STORY of the LOAVES and FISHES

Written by Alice Joyce Davidson
Illustrated by Victoria Marshall

Text copyright ©1985 by Alice Joyce Davidson
Art copyright ©1985 by The C.R. Gibson Company
Published by The C.R. Gibson Company
Norwalk, Connecticut 06856
Printed in the United States of America
All rights reserved
ISBN 0-8378-5073-8
D.L. TO: 313-1985

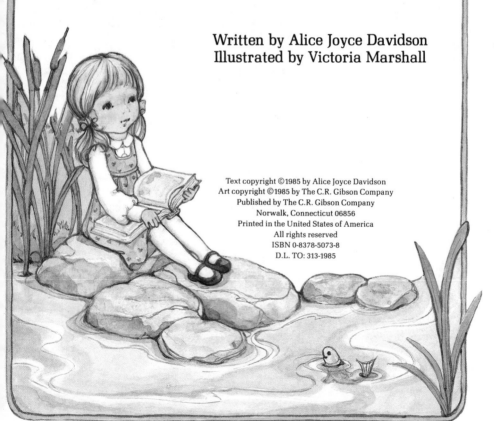

Alice had a picture book
With Bible stories in it.
She looked at it whenever
She had an extra minute.

One day as Alice picnicked
Beneath a clump of trees,
She read a Bible story
From the book upon her knees.

About some barley loaves and fishes
Was the story Alice read,
When the airmail bird dropped her a note
And this is what it said:

"Reading is the special key
That takes you where you want to be."

The picture book that Alice held
Became a giant screen.
She walked through it to Bibleland
And came upon this scene.

She saw Jesus and his disciples
On the sea of Galilee
Looking for a spot to stop
And rest beside the sea.

They wanted to have quiet
And be all alone that day,
But the followers of Jesus
Wouldn't let Him get away.

They followed Jesus by the shore;
More people joined in, too.
They came from everywhere around.
The crowd just grew and grew.

Old men came, and young men came,
And women came as well.
Even children came to hear
What Jesus had to tell.

People who were sick came,
And the lame and blind came, too,
Hoping Jesus' healing touch
Would make them good as new.

Listening to His teachings
Was such a special treat
That almost everyone forgot
To take some food to eat.

But one small boy remembered.
He'd packed a tasty dish
Of five small loaves of barley bread,
Along with two small fish.

Jesus kept on sailing
On the sea of Galilee
While the crowds kept growing bigger
On the shore along the sea.

Finally Jesus found the place
That He'd been looking for;
But He was not alone at all,
For great crowds lined the shore.

Five thousand people came that day
To listen to Him talk,
And many came for healing
For they could barely walk.

So Jesus stayed there with the crowd
He loved so very much,
And healed the sick, the lame, and blind
With His special healing touch.

Then as He talked about God's love,
The sun began to set,
And Jesus realized no one there
Had eaten supper yet.

He turned to His disciples
And asked them to buy bread,
For His followers were hungry
And needed to be fed.

"We haven't enough money
To feed this crowd today,"
One disciple said to Jesus,
"So send them on their way."

The young boy who had brought some food
Came forth and bravely said,
"I have some food—two little fish,
And five small loaves of bread."

Jesus had the crowd sit down
And said a loving prayer
To thank God for the bread and fish
The boy gave Him to share.

Then Jesus broke the barley bread.
He broke the fish up, too.
The more he broke, the more the food
Just grew, and grew, and GREW!

As Jesus broke the bread and fish
His disciples passed it out.
The crowd saw quite a miracle—
Of this there is no doubt.

For two small fish and five small loaves
Of bread were passed along,
And made a filling supper
For a crowd five thousand strong!

Not only was there food enough
For each and every one,
Twelve baskets filled with food were left
When everyone was done.

And all who saw the miracle
That Jesus worked that day
Agreed God's promised Savior
At last had come their way.

The time had come for Alice
To leave that Bible scene.
She came back home by walking through
Her very special screen.

Alice went back to her house
And put her book away
And thought, "I learned so very much
In Bibleland today."

"I saw Jesus healing those who hurt
And teaching folks God's way,
And watched a boy who'd listened well
Share all he had that day."

"His meal was small, the crowd was big,
But he was glad to give
All he had to Jesus
Who'd taught him how to live."

"I found out, too, the miracle
That Jesus did that day
Showed He was the Promised One
Whom God had sent our way."

"And finally I learned to put
My trust in God above,
For He provides for everyone
And shares His endless love!"